In a Rainforest Tree

Contents

Written by Liz Miles

Collins

The Amazon rainforest is damp and hot.
A lot is hidden by the treetops.

mist

Shall we see what is in just one tree?

At the bottom

You can **track** ant trails at the bottom of the tree.

This animal hunts ants. It must be quick ... some ants sting!

Insects, slugs and snails feed by the trunk.

This snail is as big as a hand!

Some **scarabs**, like this one, feed on animal dung.

Up the trunk

Big cats sleep up the trunk. The treetop **screens** the sun.

This animal waits to hunt a rat.
Its **fangs** inject **venom**.

Tree frogs cling on with pads. They creep to the wettest spots on the trunk.

pads

This waits unseen ... then feeds on a frog!

In the treetop

Lots of animals hang from the treetop.
Some have long, strong tails to swing from.

They jump from tree to tree.

There is a lot to feed on in the treetop.
This animal creeps along, munching twigs.

This big bill can crack nuts and seeds.

At the top

Some trees stick out at the top of the rainforest.

parrots

Throngs of bees buzz in nests up here.

nest

17

Keep the trees!

There is so much to see in an Amazon rainforest tree.

Animals and insects need the trees so they
can exist.

Glossary

fangs long teeth

scarabs bugs

screens stops the sun from getting in

throngs lots of

track seek out

venom toxic liquid that can kill an animal

Index

Rainforest tree

At the top

In the treetop

Up the trunk

At the bottom

After reading

Letters and Sounds: Phases 3 and 4

Word count: 233

Focus phonemes: /ch/ /sh/ /th/ /ng/ /ai/ /ee/, and adjacent consonants

Common exception words: of, to, the, by, we, be, you, they, have, like, so, some, there, one, out, what, here

Curriculum links: Science: Living things and their habitats

National Curriculum learning objectives: Reading/word reading: read accurately by blending sounds in unfamiliar words containing GPCs that have been taught; read common exception words, noting unusual correspondences between spelling and sound and where these occur in a word; read other words of more than one syllable that contain taught GPCs; Reading/comprehension (KS2): understand what they read, in books they can read independently, by checking that the text makes sense to them, discussing their understanding and explaining the meaning of words in context; identifying main ideas drawn from more than one paragraph and summarising these

Developing fluency

- Take turns to read a page, ensuring your child pauses for full stops, commas and ellipses to add to the suspense or excitement.
- Encourage your child to read with an enthusiastic expression, to express the wonder of the rainforest.

Phonic practice

- Practise reading words with more than one syllable, breaking them up into syllables:

  rain-fo-rest   in-sects   sca-rabs   un-seen   munch-ing

- Take turns to point to a word, read and identify the number of syllables. Include words with only one syllable too.

Extending vocabulary

- Challenge your child to describe what each creature looks like. Encourage them to be specific about colours, textures and body parts, for example:
  - page 6: snail – glistening bumpy orange body and long horns; hard brown shell